PEOPLE & PLACES

Middle East

Written by

Antony Mason

Consultant Trevor Mostyn

Illustrated by

Ann Savage

SILVER BURDETT PRESS
ENGLEWOOD CLIFFS, NEW JERSEY

Editors Steve Parker, Jane Alison
Editor, U.S. Edition Nancy Furstinger
Designers Bridget Morley, Patrick Nugent
Photo-researcher Hugh Olliff
Studio services Kenneth Ward

A TEMPLAR BOOK

Devised and produced by Templar Publishing Ltd
107 High Street, Dorking, Surrey RH4 1QA

Adapted and first published in the United States in 1988
by Silver Burdett Press, Englewood Cliffs, N.J.

Copyright © 1988 by Templar Publishing Ltd
Illustrations copyright © 1988 by Templar Publishing Ltd
This adaptation © 1988 by Silver Burdett Press

Color separations by Positive Colour Ltd, Maldon, Essex
Printed by L.E.G.O., Vicenza, Italy

Library of Congress Cataloging-in-Publication Data

Mason, Antony.
   Middle East.
   (People & places)
   "A Templar book" — verso t.p.
   Includes index
   Summary: Text and illustrations introduce the geography, history,
people, and culture of the Middle East.
   1. Middle East — Juvenile literature.   [1. Middle East]
I. Savage, Ann, ill.   II. Title   III. Series: People & places
(Englewood Cliffs, N.J.)
DS42.4.M33   1988   956   88-18312
ISBN 0-382-09514-6

Contents

UNITED BY NAME

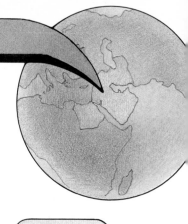

The "Middle East" is a fairly new name for a region with some of the oldest civilizations in the world. The name has become familiar only in the last 50 years or so. It describes the group of countries that stretch from the eastern end of the Mediterranean Sea, across the wedge-shaped Arabian Peninsula, to the area around the Arabian Gulf.

These lands are neither "Western" like Europe and North America, nor "Eastern" like China and Japan. In fact, they are very much at the crossroads between West and East. They have been centers for trade, cultures, and religions that have spread westward and eastward since the dawn of history.

The countries of the Middle East have much in common. They share the same hot climate, and they have many similar traditions of housing, clothing, and food. Arabic is the main language, and Islam is the main religion. Yet there is also great variety, both in the landscape and in the way that people live. In some areas people have modern houses, luxury cars, and private planes. In others, the way of life has barely changed for thousands of years.

KEY FACTS

► The Middle East covers an area of about 2.6 million square miles. This is two-thirds the size of the United States and 25 times larger than Great Britain.
► Only about one-twentieth of the land is used to grow crops. The rest is dry scrub, desert, or mountains.
► The total population of the region is about 160 million people.
► Much of the region is empty of people. For example, Saudi Arabia is one third the size of the U.S. However, its population is only about 10.5 million, about the same as the population of Florida.
► The United Arab Emirates is one of the richest countries in the world. Yemen and Southern Yemen are among the poorest countries.

Symbols of the Middle East

For centuries, traders have used camels, the "ships of the desert", to carry goods across the deserts of the Middle East. The Sphinx guards the pyramid of King Khafre at Giza, near Cairo in Egypt (page 13). It is a symbol of the complex culture of ancient Egypt.

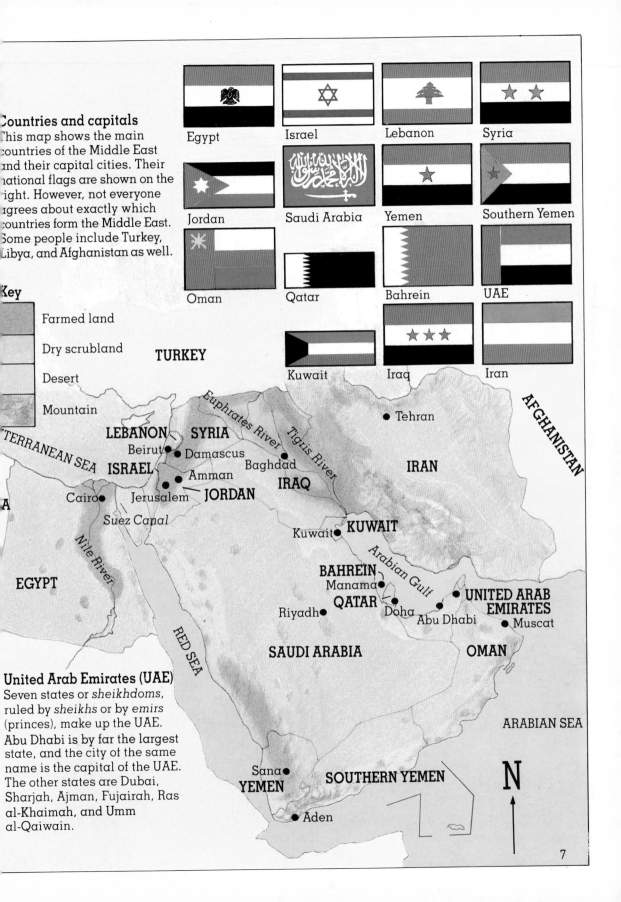

Countries and capitals

This map shows the main countries of the Middle East and their capital cities. Their national flags are shown on the right. However, not everyone agrees about exactly which countries form the Middle East. Some people include Turkey, Libya, and Afghanistan as well.

Key

Farmed land

Dry scrubland

Desert

Mountain

Egypt

Israel

Lebanon

Syria

Jordan

Saudi Arabia

Yemen

Southern Yemen

Oman

Qatar

Bahrein

UAE

Kuwait

Iraq

Iran

TURKEY

MEDITERRANEAN SEA

Euphrates River

Tigris River

Tehran

AFGHANISTAN

LEBANON   SYRIA

Beirut   Damascus

ISRAEL   Baghdad

IRAN

Amman

Cairo   Jerusalem   JORDAN   IRAQ

Suez Canal

Kuwait   KUWAIT

Nile River

Arabian Gulf

BAHREIN

Manama

EGYPT   QATAR   Doha   UNITED ARAB EMIRATES

Riyadh   Abu Dhabi   Muscat

RED SEA

SAUDI ARABIA   OMAN

ARABIAN SEA

United Arab Emirates (UAE)

Seven states or *sheikhdoms*, ruled by *sheikhs* or by *emirs* (princes), make up the UAE. Abu Dhabi is by far the largest state, and the city of the same name is the capital of the UAE. The other states are Dubai, Sharjah, Ajman, Fujairah, Ras al-Khaimah, and Umm al-Qaiwain.

Sana   SOUTHERN YEMEN

YEMEN

N

Aden

7

WATER AND SUN

Parts of the Middle East are among the hottest and driest places in the world. The sun beats down in a cloudless sky, and there are months or years without rain. Temperatures during the day often reach 105°F and sometimes rise to more than 125°F. Vast areas of the region consist of waterless desert where nothing grows and nobody lives.

The key to life is water. Where there is a good supply of water, people can grow crops, raise animals, and settle in villages and towns. This means that most of the large towns in the Middle East are next to rivers or on the coast. Some towns are in the mountains, where the air is cooler and there is more rain. Others are built around oases. These are places in the desert where underground water can be reached by wells or springs.

But it is not always stiflingly hot. The nights can be chilly, especially away from the coasts. In winter (October to April), the days too may be cold, with temperatures down to 40°F. It snows in the mountains of Lebanon and Iran.

Irrigation
Where rain is scarce, water from rivers or springs has to be taken out to the fields in pipes and channels. Complicated systems of field irrigation have been used by farmers in the Middle East for thousands of years. This tree, watered by a drip feed pipe and protected by barbed wire from desert animals, is in Abu Dhabi.

Dressing for the weather
Many people in the Middle East wear traditional, loose-fitting robes and head-coverings. Such light, airy clothes are suited to the hot climate. They give protection from the hot sun, dust, and sandstorms, yet they allow air to circulate around the body. These men are wearing traditional dress from Bahrein.

Water, key to life

Lush, green crops grow on the banks of the Nile River, near Luxor in central Egypt. Water from the river is taken by pipes to moisten the soil in the nearby fields. However, just beyond is dry, barren, mountainous desert.

The Dead Sea

This large lake is on the border between Israel and Jordan. It is the lowest point on the earth's land surface, at 1,280 feet below sea level! The heat of the sun has evaporated the water over centuries, so the salt in it has become more concentrated than ordinary sea water. On the lake shore, salt crystals sparkle in the sun (as shown here) like white beach sand. Very few animals and plants can live in the water or on the shore, which explains why the lake got its name.

WILDLIFE OF THE DESERT

Dry scrub and deserts cover vast areas of the Middle East. In the heat of the desert day the air shimmers, the rocks and sand are too hot to touch, and the fierce sun burns bare skin in minutes. Most animals are hiding from the heat, in their burrows or under stones.

As night falls, and the temperature drops, creatures emerge from hiding. Insects and scorpions scurry across the sand. Jerboa rodents and desert mice search for seeds and bits of plant food. Larger predators such as the fennec fox and the caracal cat are on the prowl.

Each animal and plant has developed ways of coping with the lack of water. Some plants, like the tamarisk tree, have roots many feet long. These reach down for moisture deep in the soil, beneath the dry surface. Other plants produce seeds that lie dormant during the drought. After one of the rare rainstorms, the seeds quickly grow, flower, and fruit to produce seeds of their own. These seeds then lie dormant again, perhaps for many years, until the next rainfall. Some places have been without rain for 25 years, and periods of 10 years without rain are not uncommon.

Desert sands

Huge dunes of sand, some more than 1,000 feet high, cover much of the Middle East's deserts. These dunes are in Abu Dhabi. Some desert areas are rocky and mountainous, while others form flat plains covered by pebbles and gravel. They all have one feature in common: lack of water. In some places the average daily summer temperature is more than 85°F.

Water carriers

These young sand grouse are well camouflaged in the desert because their feathers are the same color as the rocks and sand around them. Their parents fly many miles to find a river or oasis. They dip their breast feathers into the water, and then carry the droplets back to the nest for their young to drink, as shown here.

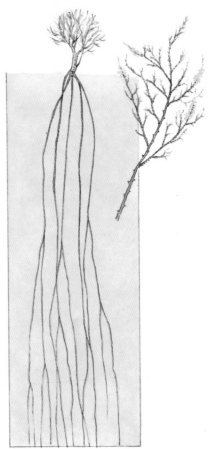

Tough survivor

The tamarisk tree's long roots reach deep into the soil for moisture. Its small, hard leaves lose little water and the tree can survive long periods of drought.

Jerboa in burrow

Sand hopper

Jerboas, like many other desert animals, are nocturnal (active at night). They eat seeds, shoots, and other plant food. They live in burrows by day, where the air is cool and moist. Jerboas never need to drink, since there is just enough water contained in their food for them to survive. Their bodies are well adapted to jumping, with long back legs and a long tail to help them balance as they hop across the desert sand.

THREE GREAT RIVERS

There are very few rivers in the Middle East, compared to other large areas such as North America and Europe. However, the three largest rivers in the area, the Nile, Tigris, and Euphrates, have been of enormous importance in history.

The fertile plains of the Tigris and Euphrates are known as the "cradle of civilization". In this area, once called Mesopotamia, small villages and towns grew up many thousands of years ago. From these developed the great cities of the Sumerians, which flourished 5,000 years ago. These people invented their own form of writing and made important advances in mathematics and astronomy. About 4,000 years ago the Sumerians were conquered by the Babylonians, who built great temples, gates, and the legendary Hanging Gardens of Babylon. At this time, too, the ancient Egyptians were building cities and pyramids along the Nile.

These complex societies had their own laws and systems of government. They traded widely and created superb buildings, paintings, sculptures, furniture, and jewelry, some of which still survive today.

KEY FACTS

▶ The Nile River is the longest river in the world, at 4,160 miles.
▶ *Mesopotamia* is a Greek word meaning "between rivers".
▶ Babylon was the capital of ancient Babylonia. It was on the banks of the Euphrates, 55 miles south of modern-day Baghdad.
▶ The city was at its richest and most powerful around 570 BC, when its famous King Nebuchadnezzar II ruled.
▶ Alexander the Great, the Greek general, spread his empire into the Middle East. He conquered Egypt in 332 BC and Mesopotamia in 331 BC. He died in Babylon eight years later.

Temples and tombs
The religion of the ancient Egyptians placed great importance on "life after death". The pharaohs and other rulers were buried in grand tombs, along with fabulous treasures. The grandest of the tombs are the pyramids at Giza, near Cairo. The largest, built for King Khufu, is 755 feet along each side and 480 feet high. It is 4,500 years old.

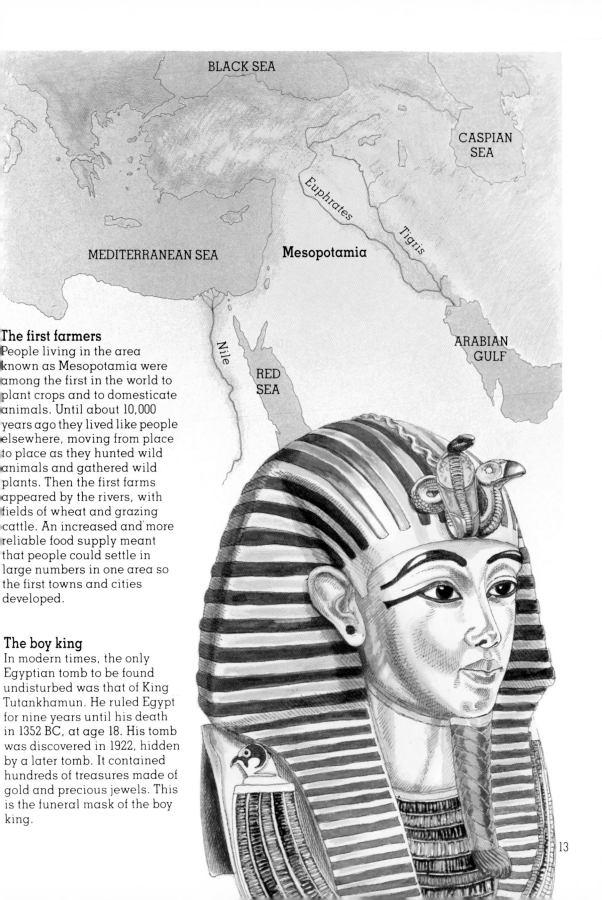

BLACK SEA

CASPIAN SEA

Euphrates

Tigris

MEDITERRANEAN SEA

Mesopotamia

ARABIAN GULF

Nile

RED SEA

The first farmers

People living in the area known as Mesopotamia were among the first in the world to plant crops and to domesticate animals. Until about 10,000 years ago they lived like people elsewhere, moving from place to place as they hunted wild animals and gathered wild plants. Then the first farms appeared by the rivers, with fields of wheat and grazing cattle. An increased and more reliable food supply meant that people could settle in large numbers in one area so the first towns and cities developed.

The boy king

In modern times, the only Egyptian tomb to be found undisturbed was that of King Tutankhamun. He ruled Egypt for nine years until his death in 1352 BC, at age 18. His tomb was discovered in 1922, hidden by a later tomb. It contained hundreds of treasures made of gold and precious jewels. This is the funeral mask of the boy king.

13

CROSSROADS OF THE WORLD

The Middle East separates Europe and Africa from the Asian continent. For many centuries, trade between West and East was controlled by people in the Middle East.

The trade routes across the seas, mountains, and deserts were established thousands of years ago. Spices, silks, precious metals, and jewels passed through the region, usually under the control of Arab traders, to be sold in Mediterranean ports to the Europeans. Cities on the trade routes, such as Damascus, Palmyra, and Aleppo, were famed for their riches and luxury. Only from the 16th century onward, when ships from Europe began to sail around Africa, did Europeans trade directly with India, China, and Japan.

Because of its important position in world trade, the Middle East has been fought over many times as various empires tried to gain control of the region. The Persians, Greeks, Romans, Mongols, Turks, French, and British all have made bids for power, and all have left their influences.

The Holy Wars

From the 11th to 13th centuries, Christians from Europe traveled to the Middle East on military expeditions called Crusades. Their aim was to try to win control of Jerusalem and the Holy Land from the Muslims, followers of Islam. The Christians captured Jerusalem in 1099, but lost control again in 1187. On the right, a painting of the time shows a Crusader knight, bearing the red cross of Christ on his shield, battling against a Muslim soldier.

Ruins of an oasis city

Palmyra, in Syria, was once a great oasis city on a major trade road to the East. During the time of the Roman Empire, in the 1st and 2nd centuries AD, it was at its most wealthy and powerful, with fine temples, palaces, public baths, fountains, and a theater. Gradually it fell into ruin and was destroyed by the Mongols in the 14th century.

Between West and East

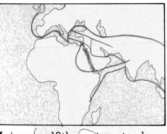

Major pre-16th century trade routes between Europe, Africa and Asia.

This map shows how the Middle East was well placed to control trade between West and East. There were few tracks across the barren land and traveling from West to East by sea meant a long and hazardous journey around Africa. However, as ships and sailing techniques improved during the 16th to 18th centuries, the Middle East became less important. Then in 1860 the Suez Canal was opened. It provided a 100 mile short-cut between the Mediterranean and Asia. The canal brought the Middle East back into an important position on world trade routes.

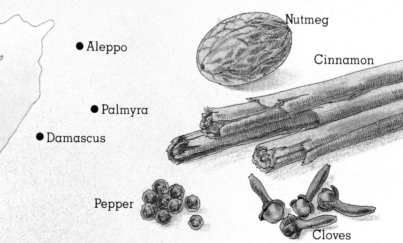

- Aleppo
- Palmyra
- Damascus
- Port Said

Suez Canal
- Suez

Pepper

Nutmeg

Cinnamon

Cloves

The trade in spices

Some of the most important goods passing through the Middle East were spices from the Far East, bound for Europe. They were bought by the rich to flavor and preserve food. They also were used to make medicines.

15

BIRTHPLACE OF RELIGIONS

Three of the world's main religions came from the Middle East. All three share the same beginnings, and each religion is based on the belief that there is only one God.

The oldest of the three is Judaism, the religion of the Jews. It developed about 4,000 years ago and was the faith of the Hebrews, or Israelites. They believed that their ancestor, Abraham, had made an agreement with God. If they lived according to God's law, their reward would be a "promised land" where they could live in peace. God's law was received by Moses and written down in a holy book, the *Torah*. This is contained in the Old Testament of the Bible. Today there are about 17 million Jews in the world.

The second religion, Christianity, is based on the teachings of Jesus Christ. He was born into a Jewish family in Israel nearly 2,000 years ago. He taught humility, kindness, and care for others, based on the Jewish scriptures. His life and work are described in the New Testament of the Bible. There are one billion Christians in the world today. Some Christian communities exist in the Middle East, mainly in Egypt, Syria, and Lebanon.

You can read about the third religion, Islam, on page 18.

Father of religions

Abraham appears in the history of Judaism, Christianity, and Islam. The Jews are said to be descended from his son Isaac, and the Arabs from his son Ishmael. The Bible tells how Abraham's devotion to God was tested when God asked him to sacrifice his son Isaac, as shown in this painting "The Sacrifice of Isaac" (completed about 1600) by the Italian artist Caravaggio. At the last moment, Abraham was told that his faith was strong and he need not kill his son.

Christian Jerusalem

Jerusalem, capital of Israel, is important in three religions. The Church of the Holy Sepulchre was built in Jerusalem in the 12th century. It is said to be on the site of Mount Calvary, where Jesus was crucified (put to death on the cross), and the tomb where his body was placed. Christians believe that Jesus was the son of God, and that he died to pay for the sins of the world.

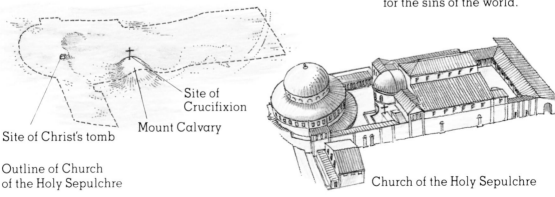

Site of Crucifixion

Site of Christ's tomb

Mount Calvary

Outline of Church of the Holy Sepulchre

Church of the Holy Sepulchre

Jewish Jerusalem

Above, Jews worship at the city's Western Wall or "Wailing Wall". It is the last remaining part of the Temple of Herod, destroyed in 70 AD. Today it is the Jewish faith's most holy place.

Muslim Jerusalem

The Dome of the Rock dates from the year 961. It was built at the place where, in a vision, Muhammad saw himself make a night journey into heaven. Muhammad was the Prophet of the Islamic faith.

MUHAMMAD, PROPHET OF ISLAM

Islam is by far the most important religion in the Middle East. Followers of Islam are called Muslims (sometimes spelled Moslems). The central figure in Islam is the Prophet, Muhammad.

Muhammad was born in about the year 570, in the trading city of Mecca (now in Saudi Arabia). When he was 40 years old, he began to feel that he was being called by God, or *Allah*. The angel Gabriel came to Muhammad in a vision and told him the "Word" of God, and that he should tell others to follow God's will. The "Word" described what people should believe and how they should live their lives. Later it was written down in Islam's holy book, the *Koran*.

At first, Muhammad had little success in encouraging people to follow the "Word" of God. In fact, he stirred up anger among members of other religions, and in 622 he had to flee Mecca for fear of his life. He traveled north to Medina. This important journey, the *Hegira*, marked a turning point. Over the next few years many people took up Islam, and Arab soldiers took the religion with them as they conquered nearby countries. After Muhammad's death in 632 the Islamic Empire continued to spread. By the end of the next century it stretched from Spain in the west to Afghanistan in the east. In 750, the capital city was changed from Damascus to Baghdad. For five centuries, until overrun by the Mongols in 1258, this city was the center of the great Islamic Empire.

The Five Pillars of Islam
All Muslims must:

1. Say "There is no god but God; Muhammad is his Prophet".
2. Pray five times a day, at dawn, noon, mid-afternoon, dusk, and after dark, facing Mecca each time.
3. Give generously to the poor.
4. Undergo a fast (eat nothing during daylight hours) during *Ramadan*, the ninth month of the Muslim year.
5. Make the pilgrimage to Mecca at least once, if it is possible.

Pilgrimage to Mecca

All Muslims must try to visit the holy city of Mecca during the yearly pilgrimage, the *Hajj*, at least once during their lives. They come to Islam's holiest shrine, a cube-shaped building called the *Kabah*, which is draped with curtains during the *Hajj* (in the center of the picture above). In one corner of the shrine is the sacred black stone, set in a silver frame. The stone, about 12 inches across, is believed to be the only surviving part of the first mosque, built by Abraham.

Following the *Koran*

Islam is said by many people to be a strict religion. Most Muslims take their faith seriously and pay great attention to the rules, so that following the religion becomes a way of life. There are no priests, but *mullahs* (lawyers) who study the laws of the *Koran* (as shown here) and *imams* who lead the prayers. The *Koran* is believed to record the exact words of God, and so these books are treated with great respect. Many are beautifully made, exquisitely decorated, and kept secure in elaborate cases.

ARABIC AND THE ARAB WORLD

The Middle East is at the center of "the Arab world" (although many Arabs also live in North Africa). Most of the people living in the region are Arabs, and they speak and write Arabic. However, many other groups also live there.

The original Arab people came from the south and west of the Arabian Peninsula. As Islam spread from Medina and Mecca, so the Arabic language spread with it. The word "Arab" is used now for people from most parts of the Middle East.

Arabic is the language of the *Koran* and of Islam. From its simple beginnings in the desert, it developed rapidly as the Islamic Empire spread. During the 8th to 11th centuries doctors, architects, craftsmen, artists, and poets came to the area, particularly to the capital, Baghdad. The language became more complex as dazzling discoveries were made in science, mathematics, and medicine. Today Arabic is spoken by 120 million people in the Middle East and North Africa.

Letters and numbers
Written Arabic is read from right to left. There are 28 letters in the alphabet, and they are all consonants. Vowel sounds are indicated by small extra lines and dots. Some of the Arabic numbers shown here may seem familiar to those who read and write English. In fact, the numbers of the English language are called "Arabic numerals" since they came originally from Arabic.

Dark and fair
Many Arabs are dark-skinned, dark-eyed, and dark-haired. However, in certain parts of the Middle East, such as Syria and Lebanon, some people have blue eyes (such as this Palestinian man) and fair skin. Many of these people are descended from European Crusaders who settled in the area after the Holy Wars. Others are descended from Turkish people.

Words, not pictures

Many kinds of pictures, especially of people and animals, are forbidden by Islam. This dates back to the time before Muhammad, when pictures and statues of many different gods and idols were worshipped. The laws of Islam said that God himself must be worshipped, and not a picture or statue of him (or anyone else). Instead of objects, graceful, flowing Arabic letters often were used to decorate metalwork, pottery, glassware, carvings, even buildings like the arch shown above. The art of the calligrapher, or handwriting specialist, is greatly prized.

A debt to Arab learning

The artists, scholars, and scientists of the European Renaissance period owe much to Arab learning. They took many of their ideas, inventions, and practical skills from people of the Middle East, who had developed them centuries before, and from Arabic translations of the writings of the ancient Greeks. This picture, painted in 1237, shows a pilgrim caravan on its way to Europe.

CUSTOMS AND INFLUENCE OF ISLAM

Islam affects the pattern of life throughout the Middle East – from daily worship, to the relationship between men and women, to how countries are governed.

Each country in the Middle East has its own form of government. Some have a democratic system, where people vote for their representatives. In Egypt, the president is proposed by government members and then voted in by the people. Other countries are quite different. Saudi Arabia is a kingdom and has been ruled by members of the Saud family for more than 50 years. In most Gulf states the leaders of the ruling families, the *sheikhs*, control the government.

Legal matters tend to follow the *Sharia*, the laws of Islam as set out in the *Koran* and in the *Hadith*, the sayings of the Prophet. To people in the West, the punishments may seem harsh, such as being whipped for stealing. However, crimes of many types are less common in the region, compared with most Western countries. Islam also teaches that men and women should be treated differently. In some areas, a wife should not even be seen beside her husband in public.

Leading the change
Ibn Saud, shown here, is the "founding father" of modern Saudi Arabia. He was the leader of the Wahhabi people, and by 1932 he had brought various groups together into a single nation. By the time of his death in 1953, he had seen his country change from a loose grouping of various people into a unified Islamic kingdom.

A woman's place
Traditionally, Islam teaches that a woman should look after the family and the home. In the stricter Islamic countries, women are not allowed to be seen in public unless their heads and faces are covered by veils and their arms and legs are clothed. They rarely hold important positions in business or take part in government or legal matters. Despite pressure from some younger women (and men), these rules are often strictly upheld in many places.

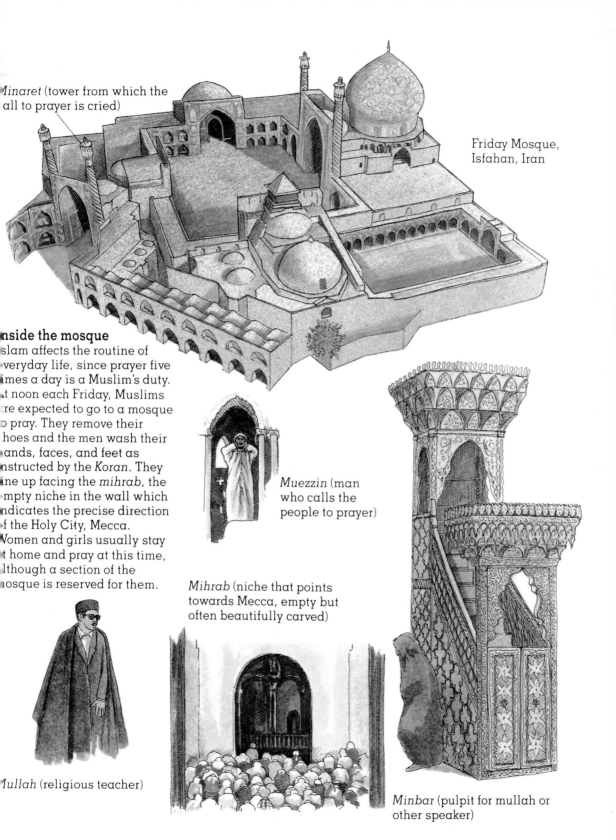

Minaret (tower from which the call to prayer is cried)

Friday Mosque, Isfahan, Iran

Inside the mosque

Islam affects the routine of everyday life, since prayer five times a day is a Muslim's duty. At noon each Friday, Muslims are expected to go to a mosque to pray. They remove their shoes and the men wash their hands, faces, and feet as instructed by the *Koran*. They line up facing the *mihrab*, the empty niche in the wall which indicates the precise direction of the Holy City, Mecca. Women and girls usually stay at home and pray at this time, although a section of the mosque is reserved for them.

Muezzin (man who calls the people to prayer)

Mihrab (niche that points towards Mecca, empty but often beautifully carved)

Mullah (religious teacher)

Minbar (pulpit for mullah or other speaker)

23

CITY AND COUNTRY

L ife in the Middle East has always centered on the towns and cities. People would come to buy and sell in the markets, to visit craftsmen or doctors, and to consult with local rulers. In times of war, cities could be properly defended against attacks.

There always has been a great contrast between life in and around the cities and life in the desert. The nomads of the desert are constantly on the move. Some live by herding camels, sheep, or goats, regularly traveling to find new pastures. Others transport goods from town to town.

These nomadic people have few possessions besides goat-hair tents, rugs, and camels and other animals. They need to be tough and hardy to survive the harsh climate. Their separate way of life has given them a sense of independence which they have guarded fiercely and with pride.

Nowadays, however, many nomads are abandoning their hard and unrewarding lives in the desert. They are flocking to the towns to find work and wealth.

The "ship of the desert"

Before the arrival of cars and planes, large areas of the Middle East could be reached only by traveling on a camel. This animal can go for up to two weeks without eating or drinking, and its broad feet allow it to walk easily in soft sand. Using the camel's strength and endurance, people could cross the desert with supplies of water, food, and goods.

A Bedouin camp

The word Bedouin is from the Arabic meaning "desert-dweller". These people live in small family groups, wandering deep in the desert with their camels, sheep, and goats, looking for fresh pastures that spring up after a rare rainstorm. In the hot, dry summer, some groups camp near towns and cities. However, their traditional way of life is becoming less common. About 20 years ago, one person in 10 in the Middle East lived like this. Today, the proportion is nearer to one person in 100. This includes about 900,000 nomads in the Arabian peninsula and 300,000 in Iraq.

Bursting at the seams

Cairo, the capital of Egypt, has a population of 12 million people and is the largest city in Africa. Every year, 100,000 newcomers leave the countryside and arrive in this city, looking for work and an easier way of life. Here the *minarets* of the Muhammad Ali Mosque rise above the teeming city streets.

Ancient and modern

Damascus, Syria's capital, was founded more than 3,000 years ago. It is one of the oldest cities in the world which is still inhabited. It was built around a fertile oasis on important trading routes. Today it is an exciting blend of old and new. This is the city's Umayyad (Great) Mosque. When it was completed in the 8th century AD, Damascus was the capital of the Islamic world.

OIL AND THE WEALTH IT BRINGS

Fifty years ago, the Middle East was a generally poor region. Today, parts of the Middle East are among the wealthiest in the world. This rapid change has come about because of the discovery of the region's enormous oil (petroleum) resources.

In today's world, oil is one of the most valuable resources. It is used to make fuels for cars, trucks, and planes. Fuel oil is burned in household furnaces and oil-fired power stations. Lubricating oils are used in virtually every piece of machinery. Oil is used as a raw material in the manufacture of asphalt and tarmac for roads, for plastics, nylons, fertilizers, and even fly spray and shoe polish.

Oil scientists (petrologists) estimate that the Middle East has more oil than the rest of the world put together. Millions of barrels are pumped from beneath the region's deserts and coasts every day. Most of it is sold to North America, Japan, and Europe. Oil sales bring in great sums of money. The oil-rich countries of the Middle East have to decide how to use this wealth, as you can read on page 30.

KEY FACTS

▶ Oil was used by the Arabs more than 2,000 years ago, to treat leather and in boat building.
▶ Oil was first produced for industrial use by Saudi Arabia in 1938.
▶ Oil is measured in "barrels". One barrel is 42 gallons.
▶ The Middle East now produces about 10 million barrels of oil every day.
▶ Countries in the Middle East play a major part in OPEC, the Organization of Petroleum Exporting Countries.
▶ In 1973 OPEC raised the price of one barrel of oil from $2 to $34. This caused economic difficulties throughout the world.

The oil industry
A large number of foreign workers are employed in the Middle East's oil industry. For example, more than half the people living in Kuwait are from other countries. The oil-producing nations once sent most of their crude oil (oil straight from the well) abroad for refining, to be processed into fuels and industrial substances. In recent years they have built large refineries, like this one in the UAE, to process the oil themselves. This saves much money.

Pipelines and tankers

Oil from wells in the desert is sent to storage tanks and refineries on the coast. It is pumped through large pipelines such as this one in Saudi Arabia. From the storage tanks, most of the oil is shipped overseas in giant oil tankers. Some tankers are nearly one-third of a mile long and weigh 300,000 tons.

Off-shore oil

The oil fields of the Arabian Peninsula stretch out under the sea bed of the Arabian Gulf. Oil rigs have been built to find this oil and pump it out. This rig is being fitted out on a dock in Bahrein.

How much oil?

This diagram shows how much oil there is in the Middle East, compared to other major oil-producing areas. The quality, as well as quantity, of the oil is important. Oil from the Middle East is suitable for making gasoline for cars, diesel for trucks and trains, and kerosene for jet planes.

Middle East

Saudi Arabia	169,000
Kuwait	72,000
Iran	37,000
Abu Dhabi	35,000
Rest of Middle East	60,000

Total: 373,000

(Figures in millions of barrels)

Rest of the World

U.S.S.R.	79,000
Mexico	56,000
Venezuela	29,000
United States	28,000
Libya	22,000
China	19,000
Other countries	94,000

Total: 327,000

27

LIVING OFF THE LAND

The oil boom of the 20th century has brought enormous wealth to the Middle East (see page 26). Even so, away from the towns and factories, most people still live by farming the land. They raise sheep, goats, and chickens and grow such crops as the climate allows. Wheat and barley come from the damper north. Rice and millet grow in the hot south, and dates are picked at the oases. Fruits such as oranges, olives, and grapes grow around the Mediterranean coast.

Farmers in some areas are wealthy enough to buy tractors, harvesters, and other machinery. For millions of poorer farmers, however, teams of oxen pull the plows, or the people themselves hack at the hard, dry soil with picks and hoes. They carefully dig channels and keep them clear, to bring precious water to the fields.

In some areas, farmers plant "cash crops" that they sell for money, rather than eating the produce themselves. Such crops include coffee in Saudi Arabia and Yemen, cotton in Egypt and Syria, tobacco in Syria, and sugarcane in Oman. Iraq is the world's leading exporter of dates.

The traditional market
Traders have sold food and goods in covered markets called *suqs*, since the days of the great trade routes to the East. Most small towns have a market, where people discuss local affairs and business. This market is in a suburb of Cairo, in Egypt.

"I heard it at the well"

Thousands of small villages in the Middle East do not have running water. Drawing water from the well is still an essential daily chore in some places, such as in this village in Yemen. Traditionally it is the woman's job, and it can be hard work. It is used often as an opportunity to hear local news. The phrase "I heard it at the well" is common throughout the region.

Fishing the Gulf

The Arab people have long traditions of seafaring and boat building. These *dhows* are still used by some fishermen to catch sardines, tuna, and other fish in the coastal waters of the Mediterranean, Red Sea, and Arabian Gulf.

NEW INDUSTRIES

The population of the Middle East is increasing. The countries of the region are looking for new ways of developing their industries and helping their people, today and in the future.

In the countries which have oil, there is usually ample money to invest. Many industries, from cement plants to steel mills, from factories making plastics to those producing air-conditioners and soda, have been established in recent years.

Great advances have been made in farming. Improved watering systems have been built. Scientists have developed new varieties of crops and new breeds of animals that are better suited to the climate and soils. Today, more countries in the region are self-sufficient in agriculture, producing enough food to feed their people.

Tourism is also an important industry in the Middle East. Every year millions of vacationers visit Israel, Syria, Jordan, Egypt, and other countries. They enjoy the warm weather, explore the many historical sites, and experience the local customs and traditions.

Fresh water from the sea

The age-old problem of lack of fresh water has been partly solved in recent years. Money from oil sales has been invested in large desalination plants, which take the salt out of sea water and turn it into fresh water. This fresh water can then be used in factories and irrigation schemes. In Kuwait, 4 million gallons of fresh water are produced by desalination plants every day, which meets half of the country's need. This diagram shows how such a plant works, by "boiling" sea water in a series of vacuum towers and condensing the steam as fresh water.

Industrial development

Clothes, machinery, electronic equipment, toys ... many goods now are made in the Middle East, instead of being bought from abroad. This plastics factory in Bahrein is one of the many new industries in the region. Such industries provide employment for local people, and they produce goods that are sold in the country and exported abroad.

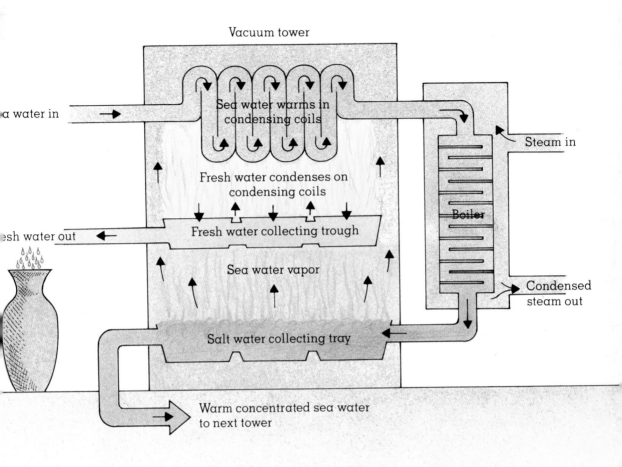

Vacuum tower

Sea water warms in
condensing coils

a water in

Steam in

Fresh water condenses on
condensing coils

Boiler

sh water out

Fresh water collecting trough

Sea water vapor

Condensed
steam out

Salt water collecting tray

Warm concentrated sea water
to next tower

Turning the desert green

The soils of some desert areas
are rich in nutrients, but they
cannot be cultivated because
of the lack of water. The money
earned by oil and new
industries has been used to
improve irrigation and "turn
the desert green". This
plantation is in the Negev
Desert, in Israel. Using modern
scientific methods, a wide
range of fruits and vegetables
can be grown, such as
tomatoes, melons, oranges,
lettuces, and eggplants.

PALESTINE AND ISRAEL

Israel is the only country in the Middle East that does not have a mainly Muslim population. Here, more than four-fifths of the people are Jewish. But this has not always been so.

Jews have lived in Israel since ancient times. However, during the time of the Roman Empire, the Romans tried to crush the Jewish religion, and the Jews fled to different parts of the world. Yet it was always their hope to return one day to Israel, their "promised land".

This became possible when the British occupied the area, then called Palestine, during World War 1 (1914-18). Jewish people went to settle there in large numbers. During World War II (1939-45), six million Jews were killed by the Nazis from Germany. After this "holocaust" the call for a permanent Jewish homeland received widespread support in Western countries. In 1948 the state of Israel was established but, as a result, about a million Palestinian Arabs were displaced or were obliged to move away. Bitter conflicts between Israelis and Palestinian Arabs continue to this day.

Finding the "promised land"
The Jewish people have always wished to live in the "promised land" offered to them by God. In the 19th century the World Zionist Movement was founded, led by the journalist Theodor Herzl (shown here), a Jew from Austria. The Zionists' aim was to make Palestine into a Jewish state. This was finally achieved in 1948.

New land, old language
After the creation of Israel, Jewish settlers from many countries arrived there to live and work. Hebrew, which was written and spoken by the Jewish people in ancient times, was chosen as the common language. However, it had not been used since Roman times. Great efforts were made to revive the language and make it up-to-date. Today, Hebrew is the official language of Israel and is widely used, along with English, Yiddish, and Arabic.

Road sign in Hebrew, Arabic, and English

Back in business

The Jewish people have established many trades, businesses, and industries in Israel. Tel Aviv, on the Mediterranean coast, is the economic and cultural center of the country. It has been merged with the neighboring Arab city of Jaffa, an ancient trading port, to form Tel Aviv-Jaffa. More than one million people live in this built-up area. This is Atarim Square, in the middle of Tel Aviv.

KEY FACTS

▶ Israel is 8,280 square miles in area, about the same size as Massachusetts or Wales.
▶ The population is nearly four and a half million. Almost four million are Jews, and 400,000 are Muslims.
▶ The capital city is Jerusalem, with a population of half a million people.
▶ The Israeli currency is *shekels*. One *shekel* is divided into 100 *agorot*.
▶ Israel has fought four major wars against nearby Arab countries since its independence. The most recent was in 1982.
▶ Some countries, especially most Arab ones, refuse to accept that Israel exists. They refer to it as Palestine.

The battle for survival

Israel is conscious of its need for military strength. Almost all Israelis, like this young woman, are drafted by the military for a year or more.

33

IRAN TODAY

For more than 2,500 years, kings called *shahs* ruled the land that people in the West knew as Persia. In 1935, this country asked that it be known by its older and more correct name, Iran, meaning "Land of the Aryans". In 1979 the last shah, Muhammad Reza Shah Pahlavi, was removed from power. The Islamic Republic of Iran was born.

During the 1980s, a strong movement of "Islamic fundamentalism" swept through Iran. More than nine out of 10 Iranians are Shiite Muslims, while in most other Islamic countries the Sunni Muslims are in the majority. The Shiite "fundamentalists" seek to return to the strict laws and values of Islam, exactly as written in the *Koran*. Many Iranians believe that the ideas and influences of the West have made some Muslims less strict, and that their traditions and way of life are threatened.

In 1980, Iran and Iraq went to war. The reasons are complicated and include disputes over borders and oil fields, and disagreements between fundamentalists and the less strict Muslims.

Despite these troubles, Iran remains a powerful and independent country. It has massive reserves of oil, gas, coal, metals, and other minerals. Industries such as oil refining and processing, iron and steel making, vehicle and weapons manufacture, and textile production are strong and stable.

Iran sees itself as separate from the rest of the Middle East, since most Iranians are not Arabs, and they speak Persian (Farsi), not Arabic.

The Ayatollah
In 1978, the Iranian Islamic leader, Ayatollah Ruhollah Khomeini, was forced to leave his exile in Iraq by the Iraqi government, which was influenced by the Shah of Iran and his government. Khomeini went to live near Paris, France. In early 1979 there was a revolution in Iran. Khomeini returned, and the Shah was exiled. Iran became a republic and a new government was elected.

The stalemate war

Iran and Iraq began fighting over the Shatt al-Arab waterway dividing the two countries in 1980. The Gulf War has cost more than half a million lives, disrupted the oil fields and damaged oil tankers from other countries sailing in the Arabian Gulf. Here an Iranian soldier in the war zone reads the *Koran*, minutes before an attack by Iraqi forces.

Fundamentalism on the march

This demonstration, in Tehran in 1983, was in support of Ayatollah Khomeini and his "fundamentalist" beliefs. It was attended by a million people.

KEY FACTS

▶ The land area of Iran is 660,000 square miles.
▶ More than 40 million people live in the country.
▶ The capital city is Tehran, with a population of more than six million.
▶ The Iranian currency is *rials*. One *rial* is divided into 100 *dinars*.
▶ The official language is Persian (Farsi).

▶ The landscape of Iran varies from barren mountains to fertile lowlands and, in the north, thick humid forests near the Caspian Sea.
▶ Iran has the fifth-largest reserves of oil in the world, and the second-largest reserves of natural gas.

MUD BRICKS AND TILES

As the Islamic Empire spread, from the 7th century AD onward, the Arabs conquered many great cities. Each city had its own magnificent buildings and treasures. The Arabs themselves did not have strong traditions of art or architecture, partly because of their nomadic history. Instead, they preserved what they thought was best in the lands they conquered. Local architects and craftsmen were used to create new buildings.

Gradually an Islamic style of architecture emerged. Great buildings had graceful arches and domes decorated with beautiful tilework. Cool, airy rooms surrounded spacious courtyards with fountains. In the palaces and great mosques that still survive, we can see how Islamic architecture earned its reputation for grace and elegance.

Traditional buildings in the Middle East can be beautiful on a smaller scale, too. An average family house has whitewashed walls made of mud bricks, tiny windows, and modest, uncluttered rooms. These houses are made with the climate in mind, which is often stiflingly hot in summer, yet chilly and windy in winter.

Mud brick skyscrapers
These buildings in Sana, Yemen, are not the creation of a modern city architect. They are more than 1,000 years old, and built in the traditional mud brick style. Shafts running up the center take fresh air to each level. A single building may house all the members of one extended family.

Simple but practical
Older houses in country areas may be very basic, but they are well suited to the climate. The flat roofs can be used for drying crops or pottery in the sun. Families may sleep out on the roof when the summer nights become very hot. These homes are in southern Iraq.

Islamic splendor

The beautiful blue tiles on many mosques in Iran help to make them some of the most splendid in Islam. This is the Friday Mosque in Isfahan. It was completed in the 16th century.

Combining past and present

Nowadays, many architects and builders in the Middle East are combining the old with the new, in a style called "traditional-modern". They take the elegance and wisdom of traditional Islamic designs, and combine them with up-to-date construction methods using steel and concrete. Even factories and industrial structures are built in this way, such as these water towers in Kuwait.

THE CRAFTSMAN'S TOUCH

Crafts in the Middle East today come from a long tradition of producing everyday objects using beautiful, highly-decorated designs. Rugs, baskets, and pottery are made with great skill and care that they become works of art.

A basket, for example, may be intended for everyday use. Yet by weaving it in patterns, using different colored grasses and reeds, it becomes an object of great beauty. Wooden doors are carved with intricate patterns. Brass trays and jugs are decorated with fine engravings. Steel knives are set in elaborate silver handles and tooled leather sheaths.

Some items produced by craftsmen are true luxuries. They take months to make, use valuable materials, and are very expensive to buy. Two workers may take six months to make one knotted carpet. Pieces of silver jewelry are set with precious stones and decorated with lace-thin layers of filigree work and rows of embossed patterns. They are as beautiful, and as costly, as jewelry made anywhere in the world.

The ceremonial dagger
The *khanjar*, or ceremonial dagger, still is considered an essential part of a man's formal clothing, particularly in the Yemens and Oman. It is often superbly decorated. Sadly, the tradition of carving the handle from a rhino's horn has helped to make rhinos very rare in Africa.

Family wealth
In many parts of the Middle East, a family's wealth has traditionally been stored not as money, but in the form of jewelry. This is especially true of nomadic people. At important events the women wear beautiful head-dresses, necklaces, collars, amulets, bracelets, belts, anklets, and other items, exquisitely made from silver and gems. These bracelets and anklets are from northern Oman.

Treasures underfoot

The skills of the carpet makers from the Middle East have long been famous throughout the world. Many homes are sparsely furnished, and fine carpets often are the pride of the place. They are put on the floor and also hung on the walls as decoration. There are two main kinds, the knotted carpet and the woven rug or *kelim*. Some knotted carpets have more than 200 knots per square inch. A skilled weaver can make 12,000 knots in one day. This mother and daughter from Iran are producing carpets at home.

The oldest craft

The skill of the potter goes back to prehistoric times. This craftsman from the Yemen is making simple water pots for everyday use. Even so, he takes great care in his work.

A TASTE OF HISTORY

In past centuries, city dwellers in the Middle East would welcome the huge caravans carrying spices, fruits, and other exotic wonders from the Far East. Cooks in the region experimented with these ingredients, such as peppers, cinnamon, cloves, rice, and eggplants. They used local vegetables and fruits, including olives, dates, and figs, and the meats of the region such as chicken, goat, and lamb. In more recent times, they added Western ingredients such as tomatoes, red and green peppers, beans, and chilies. The results were unique and fragrant dishes, still served in the Middle East today.

Simple, everyday dishes are based on nourishing flat sheets of bread, pureed beans, yogurt, rice, and vegetables. At a grand feast the dishes are a spectacular mixture of meats and spices, savories and sweets, and both cooked and raw foods. Layered pastries are filled with honey or sugar syrup, flavored with the essence of rose or orange blossoms. Fruit juices are made from pomegranates or quinces. Slices of sugar candy are filled with pistachio nuts and cherries. Of course meals include that famous drink of the region – coffee, dark and rich and bitter.

KEY FACTS

▶ Muslims are not allowed to drink alcohol.
▶ Many foods and drinks common in the West today came from the Middle East. They include oranges, lemons, spinach, parsley, and coffee.
▶ Both Islam and Judaism have rules about what may or may not be eaten. Pork is forbidden by both religions.
▶ In Islam, food prepared according to religious law is called *halal*. The laws are complicated. For example, no animals that have died naturally may be eaten, and blood must be drained away.
▶ In Judaism, properly prepared food is *kosher*. The laws are also complicated – for example, the animal must be killed by a specially appointed person.

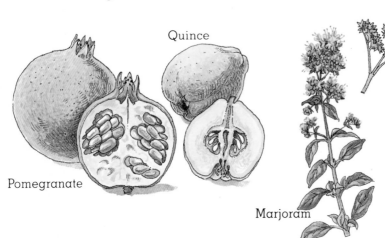

Quince

Pomegranate

Marjoram

Parsley

Coriander

Cumin

Mediterranean spices
Many of the herbs and spices native to Mediterranean lands grow well in the Middle East, and they are widely used in the dishes of the region. Cumin, parsley, marjoram, and coriander (grown for both its seeds and leaves) are all native Mediterranean plants.

Fruit of the desert

Date palms are common across the Middle East. These useful trees provide the sweet, chewy dates that are one of the most important foods of the region. Dates can be eaten fresh or dried, softened with milk or ground as flour. Date pits are ground and roasted to make a coffee-like drink, or crushed and fed to camels. Even the leaves and wood of the trees are used to provide fibers for baskets and rope. This date picker from Bahrein is using the traditional climbing method to harvest the fruit.

Honored guests

Traditions born out of life in the harsh desert say that guests must be well looked after in the Middle East. This includes providing them with plenty of food and drink. A popular way to start a meal is *meze*. This consists of a dozen or more tidbits and small dishes of various kinds, set to tempt the appetites of the guests. Here a dish of rice and lamb is served to the men of a desert camp. They eat it with their fingers, using the right hand only. The women will eat separately, when the men have finished.

41

A TYPICAL FAMILY'S DAY

At dawn the *muezzin* calls in a loud, clear voice from the loudspeaker of the nearby mosque: "God is most great ... Come to the prayer! Prayer is better than sleep..."

It has been a hot night in the modern town on the Arabian Gulf, where 14-year-old Ahmed lives. He puts on his white *dishdasha* gown and his little *taqiah* skullcap. He goes to pray with his father. Later they join his mother and sister, Leila, for a breakfast of bread, honey, and sweet, black tea.

Ahmed and Leila are taken by their father to school. They begin classes at seven o'clock in the morning. Their father goes on to work – he is an importer of motorcycles. Ahmed and Leila go to different classes, since boys and girls are taught separately. They learn the same main subjects, such as Arabic, religious studies, English, mathematics, science, drama, music, and crafts.

School finishes at lunchtime, and Ahmed and Leila go home with their father. The family eats a big spicy meal of chicken, rice, and apricots. In the afternoon, Ahmed plays soccer with his friends while Leila attends her traditional Arab dance class. The family has a light supper of vegetable stew and bread, and then watches an evening concert of Arabian music on television. It will be another hot night in the Gulf.

Not all hard work
As well as teaching new subjects such as computer science and business studies, schools in the Middle East are eager to preserve old customs and crafts. Girls might learn embroidery and traditional Arab dances, like these pupils from Bahrein.

Healthy body, healthy mind
Sports are a popular part of the school curriculum. Soccer is played throughout the Middle East, often on dusty fields like this one in Bahrein. Other sports include tennis, basketball, swimming, athletics, and gymnastics.

A mixed education
Education, like so many other aspects of life in the Middle East, is a mixture of old and new. In many countries, the money from oil sales has been used to equip schools and universities with the most up-to-date facilities, such as language and science laboratories. Business studies are also important, to ensure that the oil wealth is used wisely and new business can develop. Training its students to the highest standards is part of the country's investment in the future.

THE FUTURE – UNITY AND DISCORD

The Middle East has a troubled history. Many different people have held power through the centuries. Each new invasion and conquest brought more disputes and injustices.

Troubled times continue today. Border disputes flare occasionally, and since 1980 there has been war between Iraq and Iran. Whole groups of people fight for their homelands. They include the Palestinians, and the Kurds from the borders of Iran, Iraq, Syria, and Turkey, who campaign for independence.

Loyalties in the Middle East often are based on family or religion. In recent years there have been battles between Muslims and Christians in Lebanon, between Sunni Muslims and Shiite Muslims in several areas, and between various Christian groups also in Lebanon.

Such disputes are bound to continue. This crowded region of the world is filled with proud peoples holding firmly to their loyalties and interests. They live in the shadow of a long and difficult past, while trying to cope with a rapidly changing present.

Arab unity

The Islamic faith has done much to bring Arab people together. Shown here is Gamal Abdel Nasser, a great supporter of unity and justice among the Arab nations. He was President of Egypt from 1954 to his death in 1970. His ideas had considerable success for a time. However, Nasser's ideas have been weakened by disagreement between Arab countries and by conflict with Israel.

A war-torn land

The creation of Israel, and the ill feeling between Arabs and Israelis, has affected the whole of the Middle East. Neighboring Lebanon, once one of the most prosperous nations in the region, has been drawn into the conflict. The capital, Beirut, was once an important business center and exotic resort. Since 1975 it has been shattered by civil war.

Long-held traditions

These marsh-dwelling Arabs, from the wetlands of Al-Chebayish in Iraq, have lived a lifestyle unchanged for centuries. They dwell in reed-thatched huts on floating rafts, tending a few animals and fishing the waters. Yet around them are nations spending billions of dollars on missiles, jet fighters, tanks, and warships. Such sharp contrasts – of old and new, of peace and war – are typical of the Middle East.

Index

Acknowledgments
All illustrations by Ann Savage.
Photographic credits (*a* = above, *b* = below, *m* = middle, *l* =
left, *r* = right):
Cover page 8 Croxfor/Zefa; page 9 *a* Schloz/Zefa, *b* Braun/Zefa;
page 11 Croxford/Zefa; page 12 jacket; page 17 *a* The Bridgeman
Art Library, *bl*Biedermann/Zefa, *br* Praedel/Zefa; page 19
a Robert Harding Picture Library, *b* Zefa; page 20 Hutchison
Library; page 21 Michael Holford; page 25 *a* Gunter Heil/Zefa,
b Kasper/Zefa; page 26 Croxford/Zefa; page 27 *l* Nowak/Zefa, *r*
Moloney/Zefa; page 29 jacket; page 30 Tom Sheppard/Robert
Harding Picture Library; page 31 Braun/Zefa; page 33 *a* Zefa,
b Hilly Janes/Hutchison Library; page 35 *l* Gamma, *r* Network;
page 37 *a* Robert Harding Picture Library, Sarah
Errington/Hutchison Library; page 41 jacket; page 43 *a* Robert
Harding Picture Library, *b* Berssenbr/Zefa; page 45 *a* Kaspar/
Zefa, *b* Goebel/Zefa.